I Can See My Shadow

Lesley Pether

I can see my shadow.
My shadow is long in the morning.
The sun has just come up.

My shadow is short
in the middle of the day.
The sun is right above.

My shadow is long
at the end of the day.
The sun is going down.

My shadow is gone.
It's getting dark.